PRIVATE EYE
THE BOOK OF COVERS

CELEBRATING
1000
ISSUES

Published in Great Britain by
Private Eye Productions Ltd
6 Carlisle Street, London W1V 5RG

© 2000 Pressdram Ltd
ISBN 1 901784 17 7
Hardback 1 901784 18 5
Designed by Bridget Tisdall
Printed in England by
Ebenezer Baylis & Son Ltd, Worcester

2 4 6 8 10 9 7 5 3 1

PRIVATE EYE

Vol I Nº I   Friday 25ᵗʰ October   Price 6ᵈ

CHURCHILL CULT NEXT
FOR PARTY AXE?

contents

Butler for Gambia?

by Pravdaman Edouvard Khrankschov

YOU'VE BEEN SOLD A DUMMY

- of what we hope, after further experiment, will be a weekly newspaper to appear regularly in the New Year.

IF YOU HAVE ANYTHING TO OFFER

money, advice, goodwill or even contributions

CONTACT THE EDITOR, PRIVATE EYE, 28, Scarsdale Villas, London W8.

Sensation follows sensation in the campaign to isolate the "anti-Party group" inaugurated at the recent 22nd Party Congress at Brighton. The latest, and most startling move is Selwyn Lloyd's 'public confession' that he must "share the blame" for the current economic crisis.

Perhaps more ominous, however, is the series of articles by new Party Boss and Praesidium Leader Ivan MacLeod in the Party organ The Sunday Times, in which he is rehabilitating the reputation of ex-Premier Chamberlain.

Chamberlain was in the doghouse throughout the Churchill era, for his pre-war "appeasement" policy at the time of the notorious Anglo-German Pact. The Munich Pact is now viewed in top Party circles as a heroic attempt to buy time from Hitler before a war which Chamberlain saw was inevitable.

Purge

Obviously this campaign can only mean further humiliation for the man who ousted Chamberlain, ex-Premier Winston Churchill, and all those associated with him. Premier Macmillan has already relegated many of those who rose to power in the Churchill era to minor diplomatic and industrial posts, but hitherto the Churchill Cult itself has remained virtually inviolate.

(continued on page 2.)

BORE of the WEEK (back page)

First ever cover.

PRIVATE EYE

incorporating THE FLESH'S WEEKLY

VOL I No 4   Wednesday 7th February 1962   Price 6d.

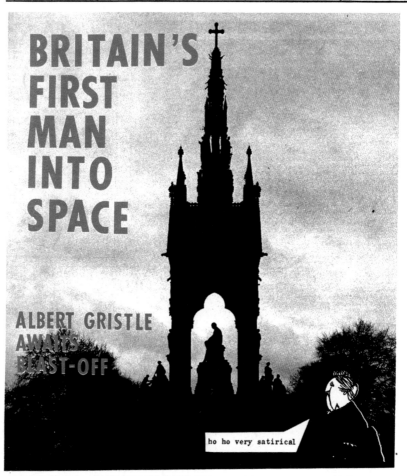

First bubble cover.

PRIVATE EYE

A FORTNIGHTLY LAMPOON

Vol. I No. 9   Thursday 19th. April 1962   Price 1/-

Britain and U.S. continue with nuclear tests.

Official opening of Coventry cathedral.

PRIVATE EYE

No. 16
Friday
27 July 62

Price 1/-

Selwyn Lloyd, Chancellor of the Exchequer,
dismissed in Macmillan purge.

PRIVATE EYE

No. 29
Friday
25 January 63

Price 1/-

De Gaulle vetoes Britain's bid to join
the Common Market.

PRIVATE EYE

Price 1/-

Minister of Defence John Profumo talks to
colleague Geoffrey Rippon.

PRIVATE EYE

No 46
Friday
20 Sept. 63

Price 1/-

Publication of the Denning Report on
the Profumo affair.

PRIVATE EYE

No 49
Friday
1 Nov. 63

Price 1/-

In the autumn tranquillity of his days while the golden leaves fall silently to the ground an old man, his faithful wife by his side, sits peacefully in the park happy in the knowledge of a lifetime's work well done, a country served and an old colleague stabbed ruthlessly in the back...

Macmillan resigns.
'Old colleague' is R.A. Butler.

John Bloom, the washing machine king, in trouble
over package holiday scheme.

PRIVATE EYE

No 75
Friday
30 October 64

1/6

QUEEN OPENS PARLIAMENT

HOW MANY POOVES ARE THERE IN WILSON'S GOVERNMENT? see page 3.

The Queen reads speech for Wilson's
first Labour government.

No 77
Friday
27 November 64

1/6

N.S.M.A.P.M.A.F.C.K.U.P. (SEE P. 13)

HAROLD DRIES UP AT LAST

I wish you'd do this when there AREN'T any photographers around

MRS.WILSON'S DIARY
SEE PAGE 14

Wilson publicity stresses humble home life.

Wilson gives uncritical support to U.S. Vietnamese policy.

First Royal visit to Germany since the war.

PRIVATE EYE

No. 124
Friday
17 Sept. 66

1/6

VERWOERD

A NATION MOURNS

Assassination of South African premier Dr Verwoerd.

PRIVATE EYE

No. 141.
Friday
12 May 67

1/6

COMMON MARKET

THE GREAT DEBATE BEGINS

Wilson calls for a 'Great Debate' on the Common Market.

PRIVATE EYE

No. 176
Friday
13 Sept. '68

1/6

GOODBYE DOLLY !

We must leave you out

Coloured cricketer Basil D'Oliveira (*right*)
refused admission to South Africa.

PRIVATE EYE

No. 179
Friday
25 Oct. '68

1/6

BEATLE HELD

SENSATION

★ SPECIAL REVOLTING ISSUE

All human filth is here
(including Robert Maxwell)

Beatle John Lennon on drugs charge.

PRIVATE EYE

No. 180
Friday
8 Nov. '68

1/6

Jackie Kennedy marries Greek shipping magnate.

Enoch Powell launches crusade against coloured immigrants.

Ronnie and Reggie Kray sentenced to life imprisonment.

PRIVATE EYE

No. 197
Friday
4 July 69

2/-

The Queen is acclaimed for her performance in
a television documentary.

PRIVATE EYE

No. 202
Friday
12 Sept. 69

2/-

Ulster's Bernadette Devlin visits America.

THE
1970s

No. 220
Friday
22 May '70

2/-

General Election 1970, won by Edward Heath.

No. 226
Friday
14 Aug. '70.

2/-

Rumours of disharmony at Kensington Palace.

PRIVATE EYE

No. 246
Friday
21 May '71

10p

Mick Jagger weds Bianca in France.
(*Byrrh is a French liqueur.*)

Visit to Britain of Japanese Emperor.

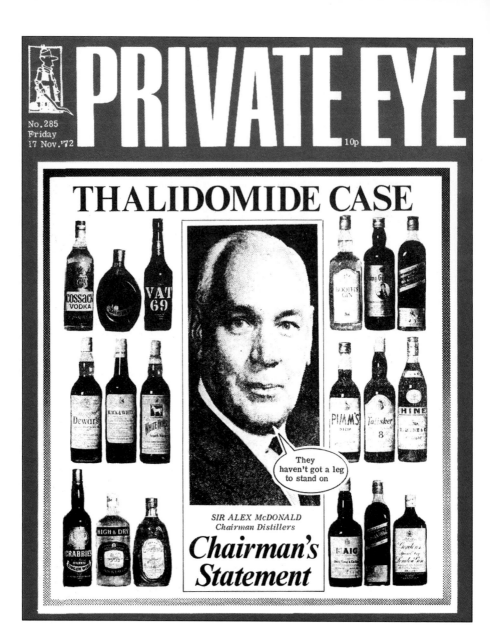

Thalidomide victims sue Distillers Co.

Cyril Smith (*left*) elected for Rochdale.

PRIVATE EYE

No. 325
Friday
31 May '74

12p

IT'S LADY SLAGHEAP!

WILSON'S SHOCKER

Marcia Williams given life peerage.

I.R.A. funeral procession in Kilburn.

PRIVATE EYE

No. 340
Friday
10 Jan. '75

12p

BRITAIN SOLD SHOCK

New Man at Palace

Arab influence grows.

PRIVATE EYE

No.353
Friday
27 June '75

15p

President Amin makes joke.

PRIVATE EYE

No. 368
Friday
23 Jan. '76

15p

UP AND AWAY !

Inaugural flight of Concorde.

PRIVATE EYE

No. 371
Friday
5 March '76

15p

Reports of Princess Margaret's romance with
playboy Roddy Llewellyn.

PRIVATE EYE

No.373
Friday
2 April '76

15p

END OF AN ERA

Alright, Jim,
you can take
over now

Harold Wilson resigns.

PRIVATE EYE

No. 376
Friday
14 May '76

15p

THORPE
RESIGNS SHOCK

Jeremy Thorpe, Liberal leader, resigns.

No.416
Friday
25 Nov.'77

25p

PRIVATE EYE

WIND OF CHANGE IN MIDDLE EAST

I hope there isn't going to be a split

President Sadat makes historic trip to Israel.

Jim Callaghan calls a General Election.

Mrs Thatcher wins the Election for the Conservatives.

Jeremy Thorpe acquitted of 'conspiracy to murder' charge.

Sir Anthony Blunt exposed as Soviet agent.

Willie Rushton's drawing shows *Private Eye* characters.

PRIVATE EYE

No. 534
Friday
4 June '82

35p

POPE'S VISIT
SOUVENIR ISSUE

It's not for me. It's for my daughter

Pope John-Paul II visits Britain.

The Thatchers visit the Falklands.

Labour leader Michael Foot comes under fire.

Foreign Secretary Francis Pym is sacked.

Cecil Parkinson 'resigns' as Minister for Trade
following 'love child' scandal.

No. 580
Friday
9 March '84

40p

Wedgwood Benn returns to Parliament as
member for Chesterfield.

Mark Thatcher goes to work in America.

The birth of Prince Henry (Harry).

PRIVATE EYE

No. 604
Friday
8 Feb. '85

40p

The miners' strike draws to a close.

PRIVATE EYE

No. 613
Friday
14 June '85

40p

Mrs Thatcher is interviewed by David Frost.

PRIVATE EYE

No. 615
Friday
12 July '85

40p

GERMAN'S WIMBLEDON TRIUMPH

Is it true about you having a lover?

Nein!

Not that many surely?

Allegations surface about Princess Michael of Kent.

The Conservative Party attempts to project a more compassionate image.

England are knocked out of the World Cup.

PRIVATE EYE

No. 641
Friday
11 July '86

45p

The Church of England debates the ordination of women.

PRIVATE EYE

No. 643
Friday
8 Aug. '86

45p

Commonwealth summit opens.

PRIVATE EYE

No. 651
Friday
28 Nov. '86

45p

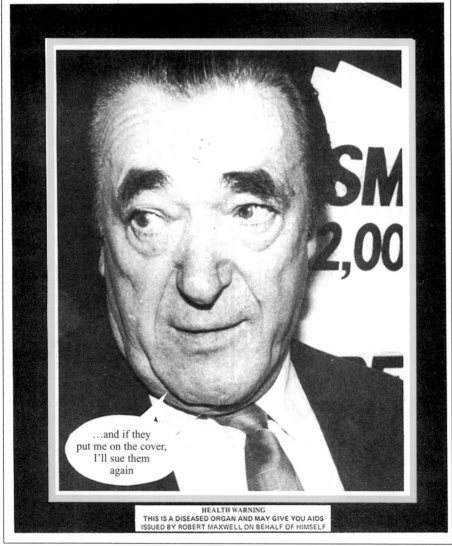

Robert Maxwell sues *Private Eye*. The *Eye* reacts
with suitable penitence.

Neil Kinnock spells out a new policy direction.

PRIVATE EYE

No. 668
Friday
24 July '87

45p

Jeffrey Archer wins libel action against the *Star* newspaper,
despite prostitute Monica Coghlan's claims.

PRIVATE EYE CATCHER

No. 669
Friday
7 Aug. '87

50p

LATEST
LATEST
LATEST
LATEST
LATEST

The Law Lords vote to ban Peter Wright's *Spycatcher*.

PRIVATE EYE

No. 671
Friday
4 Sept. '87

50p

FOURTH PARTY SETS SAIL

Owen forms 'breakaway' SDP.

PRIVATE EYE

No. 679
Friday
25 Dec. '87

50p

Delays in heart operations for children
highlight cuts in the NHS.

No. 698
Friday
16 Sept. '88

PRIVATE EYE

50p

The Gibraltar Inquest questions the role of the SAS.

PRIVATE EYE

No. 722
Friday
18 Aug. '89

60p

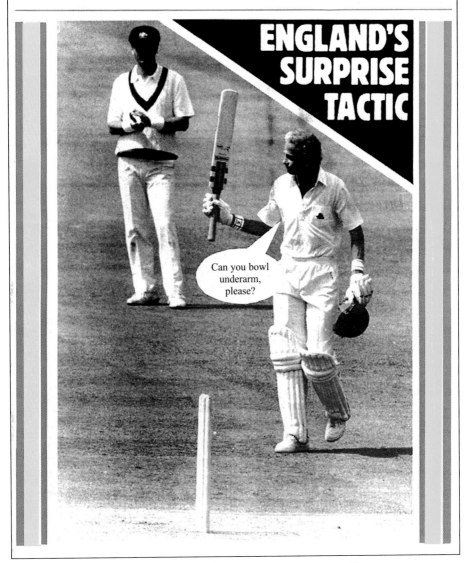

ENGLAND'S
SURPRISE
TACTIC

Can you bowl underarm, please?

The English cricket team is repeatedly
beaten by the Australians.

PRIVATE EYE

No. 722
Friday
15 Sept. '89

60p

ROYAL SEPARATION
SOUVENIR SPECIAL 1973~1989

Princess Anne and Captain Mark Phillips formally
announce the end of their marriage.

THE
1990s

PRIVATE EYE

No. 732
Friday
5 Jan. '90
60p

IT'S CIAO-SESCU !!

MEMORIAL ISSUE

When Romanian dictator Nicolae Ceausescu is overthrown, Britain
is reminded that the Queen awarded him the KCMG.

John Gummer feeds a burger to his daughter.

The Queen Mother celebrates her 90th birthday.

Mrs Thatcher is deposed.

PRIVATE EYE

No. 762
Friday
1 March '91

70p

Saddam Hussein refuses to give up Kuwait.

PRIVATE EYE

70p

No. 777
Friday
27 Sept. '91

CAREY RIOT SHOCK

The Archbishop of Canterbury attributes the recent riots
to failings in economic and social policy.

No. 786
Friday
31 Jan. '92

The Duchess of York receives more
unfavourable press coverage.

No. 798
Friday
17 July '92

PRIVATE EYE

80p

BOTTOMLEY'S HEALTH WARNING

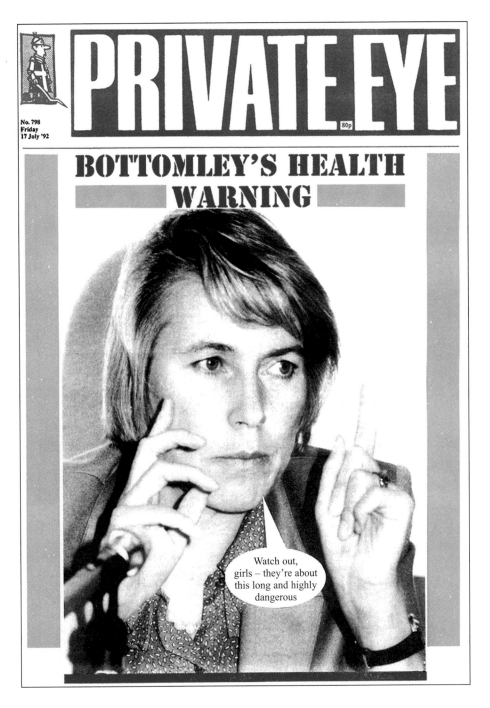

Watch out, girls – they're about this long and highly dangerous

Virginia Bottomley admits that she was a young single mother.

David Mellor poses for a family photograph after his affair with actress Antonia de Sancha threatens his career.

The press publishes intimate photographs of the
Duchess of York and John Bryan.

An unhappy Conservative conference.

CAMILLAGATE LATEST

Tape recordings of a phone conversation between the
Prince of Wales and Lady Camilla Parker-Bowles are made public.

No. 818
Friday
23 April '93

PRIVATE EYE

80p

BOSNIA
MAJOR GETS TOUGH

More trouble in Bosnia.

Listening devices are allegedly placed in Buckingham Palace.

The President answers his critics.

PRIVATE EYE

No. 854
Friday
9 Sept. '94

90p

PEACE IN OUR TIME

Another step in the tortuous Northern Ireland
peace process.

The Prime Minister faces a leadership challenge.

Imran Khan and Jemima Goldsmith announce their
engagement and her conversion to Islam.

PRIVATE EYE

No. 890
Friday
26 Jan. '96

£1

MAXWELLS CELEBRATE
ACQUITTAL

The Serious Fraud Office's prosecution of Ian and
Kevin Maxwell comes to nothing.

The BSE crisis continues.

No. 908
Friday
4 Oct. '96

PRIVATE EYE

£1

NEW LABOUR PLEDGE

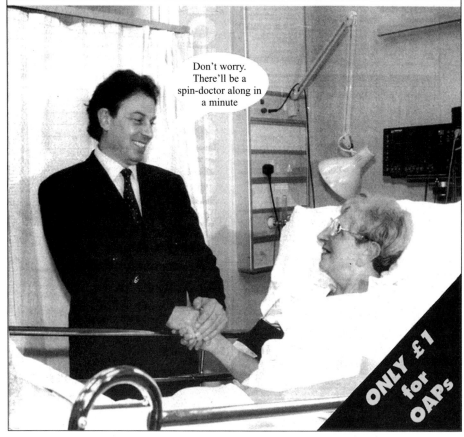

Labour leader Tony Blair's pre-election campaign
focuses on health.

No. 911
Friday
15 Nov. '96

PRIVATE EYE

£1

IT'S THE
PRODIGAL GAZZA!

Footballer Paul Gascoigne beats up his wife but is forgiven by the media after an England victory.

No. 921
Friday
4 April '97

PRIVATE EYE

£1

HAMILTON'S SLEAZE SHOCKER

What would it take to make you resign?

About ten grand in a brown envelope

Hamilton is accused of accepting cash for questions from Mohamed Fayed.

Tony Blair wins overwhelming victory in
the General Election.

No. 930
Friday
8 Aug. '97

PRIVATE EYE £1

FOREIGN AFFAIRS SHOCK

Robin Cook, the Foreign Secretary, leaves his wife
for his mistress.

The death of Diana.

Fayed continues his campaign for a British passport.

PRIVATE EYE

No. 950
Friday
15 May '98

ARMS ROW LATEST

Sierra Leone? I've been far too busy discussing Uganda

Foreign Secretary Robin Cook denies any knowledge of the Arms to Sierra Leone affair.

PRIVATE EYE

No. 954
Friday
10 July '98

£1

The marching season in Northern Ireland.

Prescott urges the nation to use alternative transport.

President Clinton denies perverting the course of justice.

No. 957
Friday
21 Aug. '98

£1

PEACE PROCESS ON COURSE

Despite the Omagh bombing, the peace process continues.

PRIVATE EYE

No. 960
Friday
2 October '98

£1

BLAIR CALLS FOR UNITY

There's a leftie — chuck him out!

Unprecedented levels of security at the Labour party annual conference.

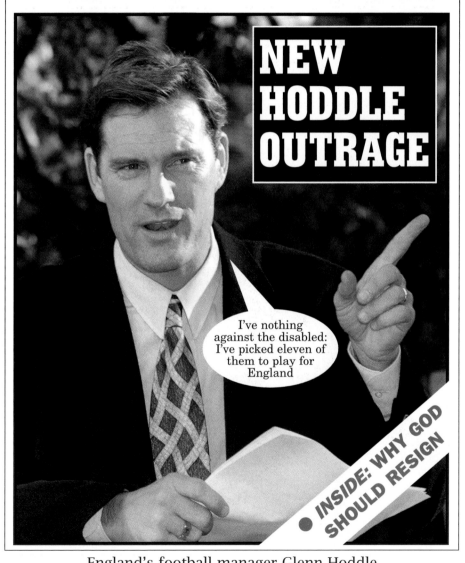

England's football manager Glenn Hoddle
is forced to resign.

PRIVATE EYE

No. 970
Friday
19 Feb. '99

£1

GENETICALLY MODIFIED FOOD
BLAIR SPEAKS OUT

> There is absolutely no danger at all

The government defends GM food.

PRIVATE EYE

No. 979
Friday
25 June '99

£1

RESERVOIR NOBS

ROYAL WEDDING
SOUVENIR ISSUE

Prince Edward weds Sophie Rhys-Jones.

No. 987
Friday
15 October '99

PRIVATE EYE

£1

RAILTRACK DISASTER
– MILLIONS LOST –

We regret to announce the cancellation of the gravy train

The Paddington rail crash leads to calls for expensive safety improvements, threatening Railtrack's profitability.

No. 990
Friday
26 Nov. '99
£1

PRIVATE EYE

GOODBYE TO LONDON
ARCHER QUITS

Tory mayoral candidate Jeffrey Archer stands down.

No. 993
Friday
14 Jan. 2000
£1.20

PRIVATE EYE

£790 million millennium dome opens.